**Note**

Companion volumes about our national government by Earl
Schenck Miers are THE WHITE HOUSE AND THE PRESI-
DENCY and THE CAPITOL AND OUR LAWMAKERS.

# Contents

A fingerprint expert marks points of identification on latent and inked fingerprints
which will be used as evidence in a court
trial. (Color photo on page 1.)

D1400944

**All photographs courtesy Federal Bureau of Investigation, Washington, D. C.**

## The Hollow Nickel

"I'm collecting," Jimmy said.

The woman who opened the door at 3403 Foster Avenue in Brooklyn, New York smiled with pleasant recognition at the boy who delivered the *Daily Eagle*. The date was June 22, 1953, a Monday. As so often happens when newsboys come "collecting," neither Jimmy nor his customer had the right change, but a neighbor finally supplied the proper amount and Jimmy went on his way, a happy young businessman.

When a boy "serves" papers, as Jimmy did, the fun is in the money he makes. He likes to jingle the coins in his pocket. If, all at once, a coin seems to have a "peculiar ring," Jimmy will know it, probably with a sickening feeling in his stomach over having been "gypped."

On that June night, among the coins Jimmy had collected, one seemed suspiciously light when he balanced the five-cent piece on the middle finger of his left hand. The coin dropped to the floor and fell apart!

If Jimmy was sore, no one could blame him. But then, Jimmy also was fascinated, for when the two sides of his worthless nickel separated, a small strip of film was revealed. Jimmy talked — what newsboy wouldn't? And a story as unusual as this was certain to be repeated: by a girl Jimmy knew; by her father, who happened to be a police officer; by a detective, in whom he confided. The detective secured both halves of the nickel and the microphotograph; with good sense, he sent them to the New York office of the Federal Bureau of Investigation.

In time Jimmy's "hollow nickel" and

# THE STORY OF
# THE F.B.I.

Written by Earl Schenck Miers

Editorial Production: Donald D. Wolf     Design and Layout by Margot L. Wolf

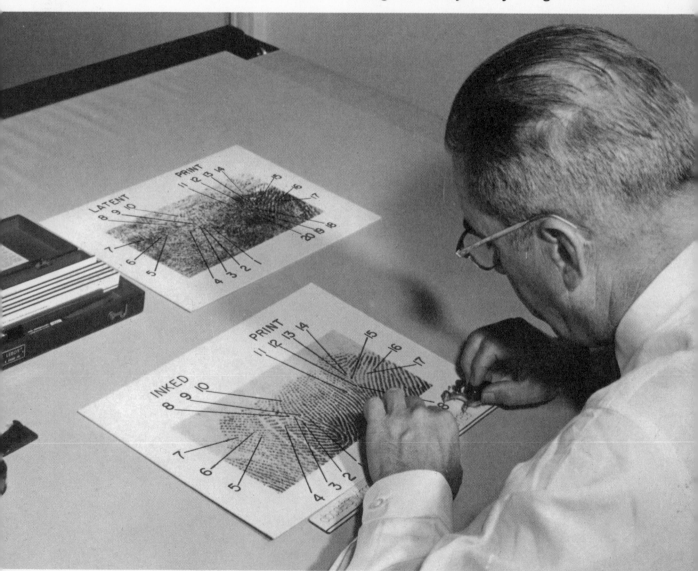

**WONDER BOOKS · NEW YORK**
A Division of GROSSET & DUNLAP, Inc.

Assuming the kneeling ("double-action") firing position, a special agent of the FBI prepares to test his marksmanship with a pistol at the bureau's range in Quantico, Virginia.

Library of Congress Catalog Card Number: 65-21505

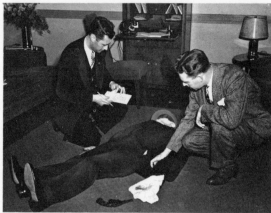

The FBI Training School has a "crime scene" room where hypothetical crimes take place and where agents are instructed in proper examination and criminal investigation.

Tracer bullets provide a spectacular display as agents fire machine guns during firearms practice at night.

A scale model of a street scene, for use in a trial, is meticulously constructed by technicians of the FBI Exhibits Section.

film strip reached the building at the corner of Ninth Street and Pennsylvania Avenue in Washington, D.C. that houses the United States Department of Justice and the headquarters of the FBI. Here a team of experts went to work on the newsboy's mystery, but it required four years and a touch of luck before the puzzle was pierced.

Certain facts were known almost at once. While such coins are commonplace among magicians, this coin was too thinly hollowed to hide anything but a tiny piece of paper or film, thus making it worthless in performing tricks. On one side Jimmy's coin was a 1948 Jefferson nickel, but the reverse side had been made from another coin that had been minted during World War II when a shortage of nickel necessitated the use of a copper-silver alloy. On the 1948 Jefferson-nickel side of the coin FBI experts detected a tiny hole in the second letter of the word "trust," so drilled that a fine needle or some other small prod could be employed in forcing the two parts to open. The film strip contained in the coin revealed a series of numbers arranged in ten columns, but at the time this microphotograph was without meaning. Since the typewriter that had produced these figures was a make unknown to the FBI, the machine obviously must have been manufactured abroad.

As the investigation continued, other "strange" coins reached FBI headquarters — from New York City a half dollar so ground that smaller coins could be concealed under it; from Los Angeles a 1953 Lincoln penny that had been coated with nickel; from Washington, D.C. two hollow pennies. Years passed and the mystery of the newsboy's nickel remained unsolved, but in crime detection no virtue exceeds patience. One day, as this narrative will relate, FBI persistence uncovered the link between Jimmy's coin and a plot to undermine national security. What happened thereafter made America a bit safer for every citizen.

Combating espionage certainly must rank foremost among the many functions of the FBI in its day-and-night war against all the criminal elements that threaten to weaken and even to destroy our social structure. Within certain prescribed limits, the FBI has only one duty: to protect the rights and freedom of every American citizen, no matter what risk is involved or whose feelings may be ruffled. This tradition of the FBI fits an historic pattern created by a stubborn President who was quite adept at matching wits with huffy Congressmen.

## How the Bureau Began

Theodore Roosevelt — "that madman" and "that cowboy," his enemies called him — brought a burst of restless energy to the White House. "We woke up every morning," a friend of his said, "wondering what new adventure we were off on when Roosevelt was President." One of "Teddy's" major crusades in those years was breaking up big-business trusts in the East and thwarting land thievery in the West, and in both these enterprises he used Secret Service agents to good effect. In the process, however, Teddy was coming down hard on more than one set of Congressional toes; glowers turned into growls and growls into action, with the result that Congress passed a law forbidding the Department of Justice and all executive agencies other than the Treasury to employ Secret Service agencies in investigative work.

The Roosevelt neck and cheeks were famous for their flush of color under such circumstances; Teddy's fists clenched and the eyes snapped behind his gold-rimmed glasses; in the White House, as in Congress, a glower could turn into a growl and a growl into action. The President's response was to order Attorney General Charles Joseph Bonaparte to organize an investigative branch for the Department of Justice . . . and so, on July 26, 1908, the Bureau of Investigation came into existence.

In its infancy, the Bureau followed the course of all human enterprises: It had to creep before it stood erect and then stumbled before it walked. New Congresses could enlarge the Bureau's activities with the passage of the White Slave Traffic Act in 1910 and the National Motor Vehicle Theft Act in 1919, but what was clearly lacking in Congress and elsewhere was an understanding of how an effective law-enforcement agency must be organized and operated. Too often, partisan politics decided the structure of the Bureau so that "its agents were appointed not on what they knew, but whom they knew." Never was the ineptitude of the Bureau more painfully revealed than during World War I. Its "untrained and undisciplined" personnel were no match for German saboteurs intent on blowing up vital installations; German spies everywhere carried on their activities with obvious contempt for the effectiveness of the Bureau's agents.

The situation steadily worsened until Calvin Coolidge reached the White House. There was a tough side to this son of Vermont, which both the President and the country needed, for one of Coolidge's first big jobs was to overcome the stigma of corruption in government left by the "Teapot Dome" scandals of the Warren G. Harding Administration. Perhaps it was entirely within character for the flinty Coolidge to place his reliance in men of strong will. His Attorney General was Harlan Fiske Stone, later to become Chief Justice of the United States; and Stone, determined that the Department of Justice must have an investigative branch worthy of the nation's respect, found the leader he wanted in John Edgar Hoover, then the Bureau's assistant director.

Hoover at the time was 29 years old — a broad-shouldered man who did not really look the part of a future nemesis to spies, kidnappers, bank robbers and other assorted bad men. Born January 1, 1895, in the District of Columbia, he attended the District's public schools and at the age of 18 secured his first job as a messenger in the Library of Congress — again, small evidence that here walked a fellow who would grow into a legend.

The Department of Justice Building, Washington, D. C., headquarters of the Federal Bureau of Investigation.

J. Edgar Hoover, Director of the Federal Bureau of Investigation, U. S. Department of Justice.

But there was a drive in J. Edgar Hoover, a go-ahead quality that would have pleased old Justice Oliver Wendell Holmes, who believed every young man needed "a fire burning in his belly." Night courses at the George Washington University enabled Hoover to earn both a bachelor's and a master's degree from this honored institution, and he was marked for advancement almost from that moment in 1917 when he started to work in the Department of Justice. He stuck to a task; he was aggressive, plain-spoken, intelligent. The Attorney General knew the kind of man with whom he was dealing when in 1924 he summoned Hoover to his office.

Stone was no bush-beater; he came to the point: how would Hoover like to become director of the Bureau? Hoover also could come to the point: the answer was yes, but with two conditions — he must have a free hand in running the agency, and political appointments and interference must end. In later years, when both the FBI and John Edgar

Hoover became virtually a part of American folklore, Stone's pride would be pardonable, both in his choice and his decision.

The changes did not come overnight. In those days the Bureau's investigators were called "brief case agents," for they were not permitted to carry weapons or make arrests. Clearly they lacked training for their jobs, a fact that Hoover knew as well as anyone. And so he began the task of improving the Bureau by weeding out the misfits. Occasionally a politician cried that one of his protégés had been misused; the director simply did not listen.

What Hoover was really seeking in his FBI agents was a new breed of investigator — men and women willing to pursue the study and to acquire the dedication of purpose necessary to making law enforcement a career. In time he would stipulate the characteristics essential to success in an FBI agent and other effective law-enforcement officers:

"1. BE READY to serve the public faithfully and fearlessly 24 hours a day.

"2. UPHOLD the rights of every individual within the law.

"3. STRIVE diligently to secure the evidence to free the innocent as well as convict the guilty.

"4. HONOR his badge — never tarnish it with personal misconduct, on or off duty.

"5. BE COURTEOUS and FRIENDLY — for most citizens the only contact with law enforcement is to report or seek information.

"6. AVOID favoritism — race, creed and influence have no place in the scales of justice.

"7. ACT as a model to youth — help youngsters to be good citizens.

"8. KEEP in good physical condition. A healthy body and mind mean better work.

"9. LEARN MORE about the law-enforcement profession — acquiring knowledge is a never-ending process.

"10. BE LOYAL to self, organization, country and God."

# On the Firing Line

In those last years of the 1920's, as J. Edgar Hoover pursued the slow, hard task of building up the efficiency of the FBI, a wave of crime and violence swept across America. The traffic in bootleg whiskey not only produced wealth and power for an Al Capone in Chicago, but other cities, such as Toledo, Detroit and New York, also were riddled by the vice and terror of mobster gang rule. A kind of national lethargy protected these hoodlums; a man who, in defiance of the Prohibition Act, made gin in his own bathtub was himself a violator of the

Shield of the Federal Bureau of Investigation.

Seal of the Federal Bureau of Investigation.

GEORGE R. ("MACHINE GUN") KELLY

POLICE PHOTO OF LESTER GILLIS "BABY FACE" NELSON

law and so he looked indulgently upon professional lawbreakers. Stories circulated that even judges took orders from Capone when he telephoned from his headquarters in a downtown Chicago hotel; at times a daring bank robber or jail breaker seemed to acquire the glamour of a movie idol

Then in 1932 occurred a crime that shocked the nation — the kidnapping of the infant son of Charles A. Lindbergh, everyone's hero since that May day in 1927 when he had piloted a single-engine plane, *The Spirit of St. Louis,* in a nonstop flight from New York to Paris. Congress awakened with a jolt. The Federal kidnapping law of 1932 gave FBI agents authority to pursue such criminals when they carried their victims across state lines; and soon Congress passed laws not only extending this power of pursuit to bank robbers, extortionists and other major lawbreakers but also giving to FBI agents the right to carry firearms and make arrests.

With the FBI thus placed "on the firing line," J. Edgar Hoover opened his shooting war on crime in the traditional American spirit of accepting no substitute for an unconditional surrender. His enemy was as tough and vicious as human imagination could produce — hellcats like the Barker-Karpis mob, "Baby Face" Nelson, "Pretty Boy" Floyd, Frank Nash and his notorious cronies. Among the first of these mobsters that Hoover labeled a prime target was John Dillinger, a Midwestern bank robber and holdup artist.

By strict definition, when the FBI started after Dillinger, his only Federal offense was transporting a stolen car across state lines. An obstinate pursuit followed. The first encounter came at St. Paul, Minnesota, where Dillinger finally escaped after forcing a surgeon at gun point to treat his wounds. Next the FBI cornered the bandit at a summer resort in northern Wisconsin; but Dillinger, surrounded, shot his way out, leaving behind one man killed, two wounded. As once the dime novel had made a folk hero out of Jesse James, so did newspaper headlines almost distort the image of Dillinger upon occasion, but the FBI kept up its relentless chase and on July 22, 1934, tracked him down to a movie theater on Chicago's North Avenue. Dyed hair, plastic surgery to alter the features of his face, gold-

KATE ("MA") BARKER

JOHN DILLINGER

A positive identification of John Dillinger from his fingerprints was possible, even though he had mutilated them.

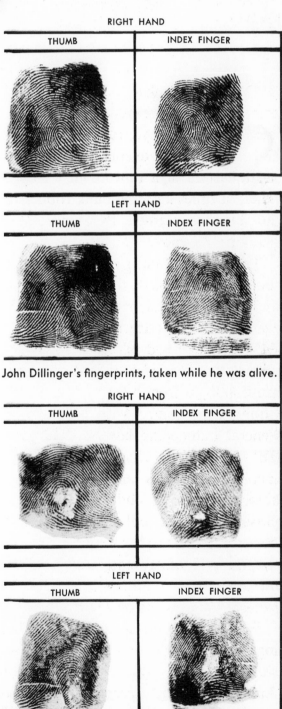

RIGHT HAND

| THUMB | INDEX FINGER |
|---|---|

LEFT HAND

| THUMB | INDEX FINGER |
|---|---|

John Dillinger's fingerprints, taken while he was alive.

RIGHT HAND

| THUMB | INDEX FINGER |
|---|---|

LEFT HAND

| THUMB | INDEX FINGER |
|---|---|

rimmed glasses, a mustache were among the devices by which John Dillinger sought to disguise his identity, but he did not mislead Samuel P. Cowley, who led the squad of FBI agents on that warm evening. They waited for two hours until Dillinger left the theater; he was shot, drawing his gun.

A new legend, a new folk hero was rising in America and another mobster — "Machine Gun" Kelly, a kidnapper —- helped to create both. Surrounded by a ring of Hoover's stern-faced men, Kelly heard the shout: "We're FBI agents! You're under arrest!" Begged Kelly: "Don't shoot, G-men!"

But for these G-men — Government-men — the end did not always come this easily. "Baby Face" Nelson already had killed one FBI agent when he was caught on an Illinois highway; Nelson shot it out with the two G-men who cornered him, wounding both mortally, but not before one put a fatal slug into his body. An FBI agent, along with an Okla-

Dillinger's fingerprints, taken after he was shot and killed, show mutilated tips — his fruitless attempt to thwart identification.

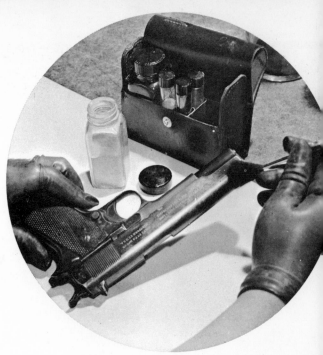

A gun recovered from a suspect is tagged with a label for proper identification.

An automatic is dusted for latent fingerprints by an expert in the Single-Fingerprint Section of the FBI Identification Division.

homa police chief and two Kansas City detectives, met death in the machine-gun battle that ended the attempted escape of Frank Nash from a railroad station. Among those in Nash's gang who got away that day was "Pretty Boy" Floyd, who had carved ten notches in a half dollar he carried, perhaps to indicate the number of victims who had died under his own flashing guns. For sixteen months the FBI followed Floyd; then, catching him, they shot it out.

When in 1936 the brutal Alvin Karpis was taken alive by Director Hoover and

agents at New Orleans, virtually an entire generation of "public enemies" had been eliminated, and a fine historian of the period, Frederick Lewis Allen, recognized the dramatic change that had occurred in American life:

"Hoover and his men became heroes of the day. The movies took them up, taught people to call them G-men, and presented James Cagney in the role of a bounding young G-man, trained in the law, in scientific detection, in target practice, and incidentally in wrestling. Presently mothers who had been noting

Shown at right are eight basic fingerprint patterns. The enlarged essential pattern is shown in color above each print.

PLAIN ARCH

TENTED ARCH

RADIAL LOOP

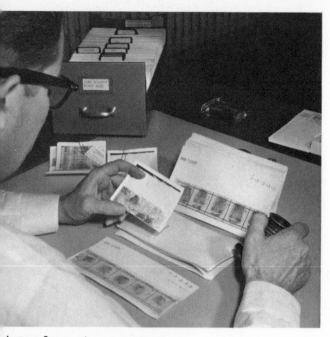

Latent fingerprints are scrupulously compared in the Assembly Section of the FBI Identification Division.

Latent fingerprints are sometimes disclosed by use of carbon arc lamps.

with alarm that their small sons liked to play gangster on the street corner were relieved to observe that the favored part in these juvenile dramas was now that of the intrepid G-man, whose machine guns mowed down kidnappers and bank robbers by the score. The real G-men — with the not-quite-so-heavily-advertised aid of state and local police — continued to follow up their triumphs until by the end of 1936 they could claim that every kidnapping case in the country since the passage of the Lindbergh law in 1932 had been closed."

ULNAR LOOP

PLAIN WHORL

CENTRAL POCKET LOOP

DOUBLE LOOP

ACCIDENTAL

# New Approaches to Combating Crime

A laboratory technician analyzes stains on an envelope that contained an extortion note.

Extensive X-ray equipment is utilized to examine castings and metal parts in the pursuit of identification and legal evidence.

Tire and shoe prints serve as means of identification, just as surely as fingerprints. The FBI's files of these prints are quite extensive, so that "tracking down" a shoe manufacturer or tire manufacturer becomes a painstaking but efficient routine.

Whereas pictures and stories of G-men exchanging gunfire with famous desperadoes captured the public's fancy, the FBI's most effective work in law enforcement in time would often occur far from the scenes of the actual crimes. J. Edgar Hoover scarcely had grown accustomed to signing his name as the Bureau's new director when he began thinking and planning how he could employ scientific method and techniques in combating the nation's lawbreakers.

A first step was the establishment on July 1, 1924, of an Identification Division. Data concerning criminals was then scattered in many places and, quite sensibly, Hoover wanted one repository where such information could be made readily available. Fingerprint records of the National Bureau of Identification and of Leavenworth Penitentiary — organizations which in the past two decades had accumulated 810,188 prints — were consolidated to form the nucleus of the FBI's new division.

The fingerprint by then had become well-established as an indispensable ally

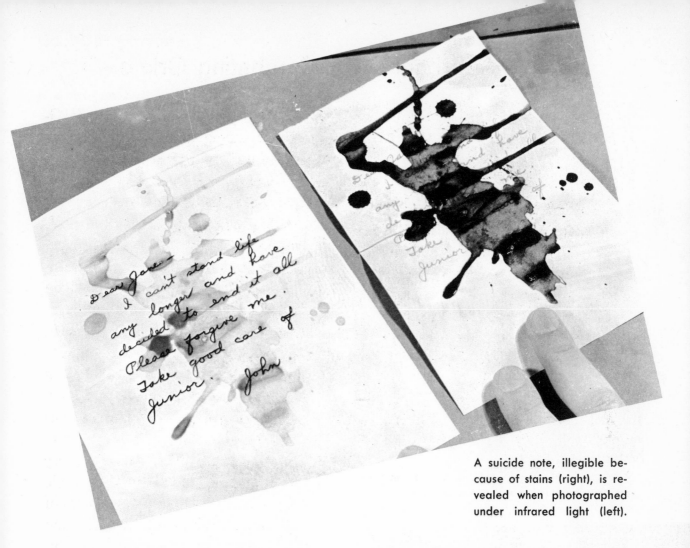

A suicide note, illegible because of stains (right), is revealed when photographed under infrared light (left).

in crime detection. No matter how quickly a criminal moved from city to city or from state to state, fingerprints were the unfailing proof of where he had been; a set of identical twins might baffle even their parents in telling them apart, but their individuality could not be hidden on a fingerprint card; and even though John Dillinger mutilated his fingers in an effort to disguise his prints, he could not hoodwink the experts. The point, of course, was the fact that as long as such prints were kept only in local agencies, their usefulness was limited; but placed in a national file, they became watchdogs that could roam the length and breadth of the country (or of the world, for that matter).

The wisdom behind the establishment of the FBI's Identification Division can be measured best by the story of its growth: In 1932 an International Exchange of fingerprint data linked twenty nations in the common task of ferreting out criminal activities; in 1939 there were 10,000,000 prints on file and seven years later ten times that number; and as you read these pages, the cards on file, reaching the division at the rate of some 24,000 a day, will be over 175,000,000. Stacked one on top of another, these cards would make approximately 116 piles as high as the Empire State Building.

And what stories these cards could tell! A traffic violator, arrested by an Eastern sheriff, could not conceal from his fingerprint card the fact that he was

15

An automatic pistol was recovered by FBI agents from a suspect in the shooting of a policeman and submitted to the FBI Laboratory, together with the bullet recovered from the dead officer's body. Microscopic markings on a test bullet, fired in the laboratory from the pistol, are compared under a comparison microscope with markings on the bullet removed from the body. This examination discloses that both bullets were fired from the same gun. A microphotograph is prepared, depicting the comparison of the bullets.

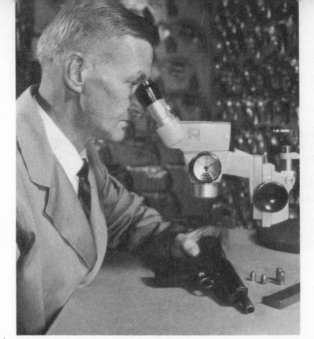

Preliminary examination of an automatic pistoi in the Physics and Chemistry Section of the FBI Laboratory.

A technician fires the pistol into the bullet recovery box in the Firearms Identification Section.

Above are photographs of the test bullet (left) and the murder bullet (right).

wanted in the South on a murder charge. An amnesia victim was identified from the prints taken when he had enlisted in the Navy eleven years before. A 17-year-old boy who left no fingerprints and committed a burglary in his bare feet was identified by the print of his big right toe. A mummified corpse, found in a boxcar, revealed his identity to FBI fingerprint experts (in many disasters, such as plane crashes, fingerprints supply the only means of identifying victims). A woman who was adopted at the age of three months was reunited with her brother after a lapse of forty-three years through the patient search of FBI experts who located the man from fingerprints made many years previously.

Fascinating and invaluable though fingerprint identification is, it represents but one way in which scientific method and techniques are used in combating crime. On November 24, 1932 a "Technical Laboratory" — world-famous today as the "FBI Laboratory" — had its modest beginning with the acquisition of some filing cases, a microscope, ultraviolet light equipment and a drawing board. Since then this scientific arsenal

in the nation's war against crime has been manned with a wide variety of specialists who can outwit the criminal by startling insights into where he has been, where probably he is going, what he has done and what he can be expected to do next. Visitors to the FBI Laboratory in Washington invariably come away shaking their heads in wonderment. Only a fool would believe that in breaking the law he could for long prove a match against this team of dedicated experts!

## The Fighting Fronts of Science

On more than a dozen fighting fronts the FBI enlists science in its war against the nation's lawbreakers. Take *firearms,* for example. The chances are good that the FBI has a model of almost any kind of modern firearm that has been employed in a crime (including weapons concealed in walking canes or an apparently harmless "fountain pen" that can shoot a gas vapor intended to blind its victim). To the FBI expert in firearms it is part of the day's routine to identify the gun from which a bullet has been discharged; and gunpowder and shot-pattern tests tell him the distance from which the bullet was fired. Nor does his day's work end here: he also can tell from the marks left by punches, chisels, axes, hammers, pry bars, drills, saws, wrenches, pliers and screwdrivers,

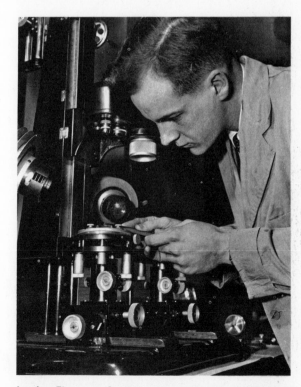

In the Firearms Section, an expert of the Federal Bureau of Investigation prepares for a tool mark examination by means of a comparison microscope.

Longitudinal whole mounts of human hair from different individuals, showing characteristic structures by means of increased magnification.

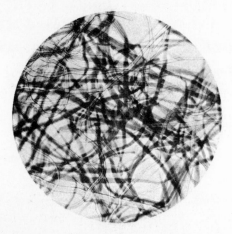

The appearance of paper fibers, as viewed through the microscope, using transmitted light.

among other devices, the exact tools criminals have used in their unlawful labors. Examinations of wood, glass, explosives and paper matches, enable the firearms specialist to place a suspect at the scene of a murder, burglary, sabotage, arson or theft.

The FBI experts in *spectography*, who may use an electron microscope permitting magnification of an object to 100,000 times its size, specializes in the analysis of paint, glass, metal, plastic, rubber, drugs and similar materials. These patient scientists, working with such apparatus as the spectrograph and spectrophotometer (instruments for photographing a spectrum or band of colored light), demonstrated their precise skill when they received from Seattle, Washington, the clothing of a five-year-old boy who had been struck down by a hit-and-run driver. Despite the fact that the lad had lain on a wind-swept, rain-soaked roadside for more than an hour and his apparel was caked with dirt and blood, FBI experts were able to identify eight layers of paint that had adhered to the clothes as a result of the collision and to tell that the outer layer of paint was bright purple. With this clue the Seattle police located both the purple Cadillac and driver responsible for the accident.

To aid in such identifications the FBI maintains the *National Automotive Paint File* which contains paint specimens of the original finishes each manufacturer places on his automobiles — an invaluable repository that often has enabled the police, working with a small fragment of paint left at the scene by a hit-and-run driver, to establish the year and make of the car involved.

*Serology*, or the identification of blood whether human or animal, has trapped more than one criminal (and also has established the innocence of more than one suspect). *Toxicology*, or the analysis of certain chemical substances, has led to the downfall of many poisoners; and in bombings and explosions toxicologists learn much from the dynamite residues. Through *petrography*, or the examination of mineral evidence, the FBI has used soil deposits on heels to place a criminal at the scene of an offense, or through mineral particles found on his clothing has placed him at the site of a burglarized safe, or through brick, mortar, plaster and dust fragments has placed him in a building where a crime has been committed. *Hairs* and *fibers* also contribute important clues in establishing the whereabouts of lawbreakers, as do *shoe* and *tire prints*. The FBI maintains both a *Shoe Print File* and a *Tire Print File.*

Since no two persons write exactly alike, the art of *document evidence*, involving the use of scientific instruments in microscopic measurements and photography, likewise has become an essential ally in modern crime detection. Among the collections maintained by the FBI in obtaining this kind of evidence are (1) a *Typewriter Standards File*, enabling the Bureau to determine on what make of machine a document was prepared (although in the case of the ten columns of figures on the film strip in Jimmy's hollow nickel the file did not help); (2) a *Checkwriter Standards File* which serves a similar function in examining checks written automatically; (3) a *Paper Watermark File*, used in tracing the manufacturers of various brands of paper; and (4) an *Anonymous Letter File*, which includes holdup notes used in bank robberies and communications from extortioners.

A fifth collection — the *National Fraudulent Check File* — surely is as important as any used by the FBI in fighting crime by document examination. As a typical fiscal year, in 1963 the

An examiner in the FBI Laboratory compares the heel of a suspect's shoe with that of a cast made at the scene of a crime. The Bureau maintains an extensive shoe print file.

Bureau received 32,381 fraudulent checks having a face value of $5,972,-697; more than half of these frauds were identified by material already on file, and approximately another 20 per cent of the frauds were identified by signatures on criminal fingerprint records.

What experience has taught the FBI is the fact that the fraudulent check passer repeats his crime, and unfortunately is a person who becomes involved in such other offenses as stealing automobiles and burglarizing stores, offices and homes. Too often, the chronic check passer is a person whose charm and in-

An FBI technician developing obliterated writing on a check through the use of iodine fumes.

telligence disarms his victim; yet sooner or later the science of persistent crime detection places him (at least temporarily) where he belongs — in jail. Forged checks have been cashed though signed by such unbelievable names as "U. R. Stuck" and "N. O. Good" — the check forger endures because he believes with the old circus man, P. T. Barnum, that "a sucker is born every minute."

The expert in *electronics* also plays a vital role in the many-sided labors of the FBI Laboratory. Not only are the radiotelephone and radiotelegraph standard equipment in modern crime detection, but in emergencies even fingerprints can be received and identified telephonically over a Speedphoto Transceiver. *Cryptanalysis* — that is, the science of examining code and cipher messages — must of necessity be a well-cultivated art with the FBI. The problems that confront specialists in cryptoanalysis can range from gamblers transmitting information on horse races across state lines to cases of espionage (remember the microphotograph in Jimmy's hollow nickel) which threaten our national security. Finally, a *translation* service permits the FBI Laboratory to handle documents written in more than twenty-five languages, including a letter from a 13-year-old boy in the Netherlands who asked for instructions to assist in form-

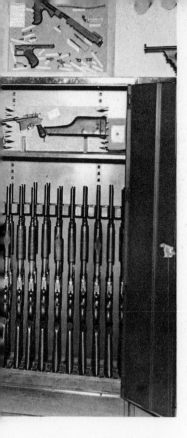

A portion of the gun vault at the FBI Academy at Quantico, Virginia. Over a thousand guns in the FBI collection are used in scientific crime detection to identify bullets and weapons in firing tests.

ing an "FBI Club" so that he and his friends could "solve secrets and other problems."

As the 1930's ended, the combination of training and science had written a proud record for the FBI. The majority of the nation's kidnappers or bank robbers either were in jail or had been executed. But by now Hoover and his G-men were involved in another struggle. Measured in terms of the welfare of all citizens, the stakes involved constituted life or death for a way of existence.

## The War on Spies

On September 6, 1939, President Franklin D. Roosevelt issued a directive instructing the FBI "to take charge of investigative work in matters relating to espionage, sabotage, and violations of the neutrality regulations."

Both the President and the director of the Bureau were keenly aware of the dangers threatening America as a result of the rising Nazi power in Germany. As early as 1926 small units of Nazis. had begun to gain a foothold in American-German communities among people who in large part and for a long time would fail to comprehend Adolf Hitler's true intentions. Meanwhile Hitler's shadow spread like an ugly war cloud over Europe; and in America his Nazi agents, working in numerous ways, sought to gain an advantage from an American reluctance to become involved in any overseas conflict.

A strange phenomenon resulted as bands of American-Germans, raising their arms at rallies in the Nazi-Fascist salute, shouted approval at speakers who spewed forth the poison of Hitler's hate doctrines. Perhaps a few realized that these American communities were being exploited as a recruiting ground for a vast German espionage system, but far more of these people were fools rather than traitors. Yet the national government knew what was going on, including the extent to which Nazi-Fascist diplomats in Washington were working to perfect a spy organization that boded no good for the free world.

Charged with the responsibility of fighting this menace, the FBI instructed some 19,000 local police agencies in methods for handling the security problems that a war would produce; and on May 28, 1940, the Bureau created a Security Division.

These were busy days at FBI headquarters. Around-the-clock experts studied the enemy's techniques of espionage and sabotage. After all, hard common sense dictated that, in the event of war, the country must be ready with a plan for moving immediately against enemy aliens.

When on December 7, 1941, the Japanese attacked Pearl Harbor, the FBI swung into action within three hours and by nightfall of December 8 more than a thousand enemy aliens considered potentially dangerous had been taken into custody. The FBI's accomplishments in safeguarding America against espionage and sabotage during World War II resulted from preparedness, alertness, a determination to out-think the enemy. FBI agents were sent on secret missions into Latin America to thwart enemy designs to use these neighboring countries as relay points for supplying submarines and spies; and espionage rings were smashed before they could begin operations.

In mid-June of 1942, or barely six months after Pearl Harbor, a strange scene occurred along the shore front near Jacksonville, Florida, and a beach near Amagansett, Long Island, N. Y. In both cases four Nazi saboteurs, transferred from submarines to collapsible rubber boats, landed in predawn hours. They worked swiftly and efficiently, for these Germans had been meticulously trained in Berlin for the tasks assigned them. The explosives they buried in the sand for later use were of highly effective quality and were disguised as lumps of coal or such innocent-appearing objects as fountain pens. Each of the eight saboteurs spoke excellent English, and two were naturalized American citizens. Among them they carried more than $150,000 in cash.

Silently they scattered, moving to points as far from the coast as Chicago. The main targets that they intended to destroy were vital to America's war effort and public morale — Hell Gate Bridge, New York City's water supply, principal railroad junctures, aluminum plants. Within two weeks FBI alertness had captured all eight saboteurs, their

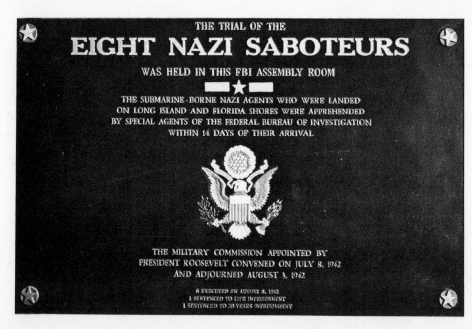

The FBI classroom in which eight Nazi saboteurs were tried by a military commission contains this plaque.

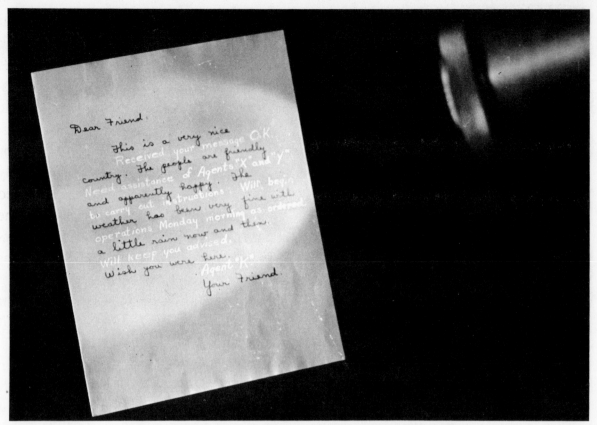

Secret writing is revealed by use of ultraviolet light. Under natural light, only the misdirecting message in black ink is visible.

explosives and their money. No single installation had been damaged.

The battle against sabotage was only one phase of the FBI's silent war on enemy subversion. With good reason J. Edgar Hoover and his G-men were often in the headlines: By breaking up the espionage network led by Frederick Joubert Duquesne early in the war, the FBI smashed the largest spy ring in the history of the United States; and when the members of a second ring headed by Kurt Frederick Ludwig were sentenced, the German conspiracy upon the American mainland was brought under a control that endured until the end of the conflict.

The collapse of the Nazi war machine strengthened the Soviet Communists so that, really, the FBI's private war on

spies and saboteurs entered a new and even more intensified phase. In a book, *A Study in Communism*, J. Edgar Hoover has identified the six principal targets against which the Soviets direct their subversive activities:

First are the areas of scientific research and development; such areas would include installations where America builds its satellites, guided missiles and rockets in addition to radar defense systems and centers engaged in projects concerned with electronics, aeronautics and atomic energy.

Next are areas vital to the nation's defense where information can be obtained relating to the methods of training our armed forces and the development and testing of new weapons.

Third, enemy spies pay particular attention to strategic areas, such as military, naval and air force installations; and to sensitive industrial sites, such as dams, harbors, railroad yards and steel mills, all places that would interest a potential saboteur in the event of war!

Again, the spy, in seeking classified information, constantly strives to "bore from within" by placing his informers in positions of trust in agencies of the United States Government.

A fifth target is associated with United States foreign policy, for the spy looks here for information concerning confidential conversations and secret documents.

Finally, the Soviet spy seeks to gather information about anti-Communist émigré groups in the United States to use to his advantage.

The war against spies often is pursued for desperate stakes, as shocked Americans learned during 1950 and 1951 when they were confronted by what the judge characterized as "the crime worse than murder." As the story of the FBI investigations unfolded, people realized for the first time the staggering dimensions of the Soviet espionage conspiracy aimed against them.

For some time before the first break came in this case, the FBI had learned that information about the atom bomb had been given to a foreign power; then British intelligence officers arrested Dr. Emil Julius Klaus Fuchs, a German-born scientist who previously had been employed in the United States on secret work involved in atomic research. Thus began the roundup of a group of widely

The staircase in the park, leading to the "bank."

scattered twisted personalities who for a variety of motives had become linked in the century's most sordid crime. Fuchs, for example, while admitting that he had dealt with the Soviets, could not identify his American contact. The FBI found that man — Harry Gold, a Philadelphia chemist—and Gold's confession led the G-men to David Greenglass, a United States Army enlisted man who had been assigned to the atomic testing site in Los Alamos, New Mexico. Gold revealed that his instructions in these negotiations came through a contact he knew only as "John," but the FBI also tracked down "John": He was Anatoli A. Yakovlev, a vice consul for the Soviets in New York City who had left the United States in December of 1946.

David Greenglass's testimony led to the deeper, if more incomprehensible source of this conspiracy. How had he and his wife Ruth become involved? The answer, David said, was the influence of

The light post appears ordinary . . .

. . . unless you know its secret.

his sister Ethel and her husband, Julius Rosenberg — they, truly, had been the masterminds. Why Ethel, who was native-born, turned from American freedom to the harsh disciplines of communism was never quite understandable to judge, jury or the public; the change had occurred during student days. It was then that Ethel had led David to embrace the Soviet philosophy; it was then through communist interest that she met her future husband. As the FBI evidence was disclosed, the enormity of the crime the Rosenbergs had incited could not be denied — the microfilm supplied by David Greenglass had given the Soviets telling insight into the construction of the atom bomb: The free world's most valuable defense secret had been betrayed.

After the Rosenbergs were sentenced to death, an American sense of fair play granted them six separate appeals before they were executed at Sing Sing Prison in Ossining, New York on June 19, 1953. In Washington and New York, in London and Paris, rallies that were not without their Communist instigators decried the "inhumanity" of President Eisenhower, Attorney General Herbert Brownell and John Edgar Hoover in permitting the death sentence to stand.

But the FBI stuck to its war on spies, knowing it was far from ended. And just three days after the Rosenbergs were executed, Jimmy, the Brooklyn newsboy, received his hollow nickel.

# More About Jimmy's Nickel

This is how the nickel looked when opened.

```
                    207
14546 36056 64211 08919 18710 71187 71215 02906 66036 10922
11375 61238 65634 39175 37378 31013 22596 16291 17463 23551
88527 10130 01767 12366 16669 97846 76559 50062 91171 72332
19262 60849 90251 11576 46121 24666 05902 19229 56150 23521
51911 73912 32939 31966 12096 12060 89748 25362 43167 99841
76271 31154 26838 77221 58343 61164 14349 01241 26269 71578
31734 27562 51236 12982 18089 66218 22577 09454 81216 71953
26986 89779 54197 11990 23381 48884 22165 62998 86449 41742
30267 77614 31565 30902 85812 16112 68312 71520 60369 12872
12458 19081 97117 70107 06391 71114 19459 55586 80317 07522
76509 11111 36990 32666 04411 51532 91164 23162 82011 19185
56110 28876 76718 03563 28222 31673 39023 07623 93513 97175
29816 95761 69483 32951 97686 34592 61109 95090 24092 71009
90061 14790 15154 14655 29011 57206 77195 01256 69250 62901
39179 71229 23299 84164 45900 42227 65833 17591 60182 06315
65812 01378 14566 27719 92507 79517 99951 82155 58118 67197
30015 70667 36201 56531 56721 26306 57135 91796 51341 07796
76655 62716 33588 21532 16224 27721 85519 23191 20665 45140
66098 60933 71521 02334 21712 51110 85227 98768 11125 05321
53152 14191 12166 12715 03116 43041 74822 72759 29130 21947
15764 96851 20318 22370 11391 83520 62297

                  № 12740/622
```

This coded message was on microfilm in the nickel.

For four years Jimmy's coin and the microphotograph it had contained mystified the FBI. Then luck brought a break in the case in May of 1957 when a 36-year-old Soviet spy, Lieutenant Colonel Reino Hayhanen, sought asylum through the United States Embassy in Paris. Born near Leningrad on May 14, 1920, Hayhanen had been a brilliant young student who, when not yet twenty years of age, had attracted the attention of his government. His work in Soviet intelligence had carried him to Finland and Estonia before he was selected for assignment as a spy in the United States. Into Hayhanen's hands were placed papers belonging to American-born Eugene Maki, including a birth certificate that identified his place of birth as Enaville, Idaho, and he executed the following affidavit:

"I accompanied my mother to Estonia when I was eight years of age and resided with her until her death in 1941. I left Estonia for Finland in June, 1943, and have resided here for the reason that I have no funds with which to pay my transportation to the United States."

The hoax worked perfectly; issued a passport as Eugene Maki, Hayhanen reached New York City on October 21, 1952, and established contact with an espionage superior whom he knew only as "Mikhail." After two years Mikhail dropped from the scene, and another superior, known to Hayhanen as "Mark," became his contact. The Soviet spy exchanged intelligence data and messages with these fellow agents by using "dead drops," or inconspicuous hiding places, such as an iron picket fence at the foot of Seventh Avenue near Macombs Bridge or the base of a lamppost in Fort Tryon Park. A hole in a set of cement steps in Brooklyn's Prospect Park was another of these "dead drops," but one of its messages was never delivered, for before it could be recovered, a repair crew filled the hole with cement.

On that "trick of fate" the ultimate solution of the case also revolved!

After five years of working in the United States, Hayhanen was ordered back to Moscow. His spirit grew depressed at the thought of returning to the harsh Communist disciplines of his homeland; a decision to defect and throw himself upon the mercy of the United States Embassy in Paris followed; and in May of 1957 Hayhanen returned to New York City. FBI interrogation about the "dead drops" developed the fact that the hole in the steps in Prospect Park once had been used before a repair crew had eliminated it; the FBI chipped away the cement and found the message enclosed in a hollowed-out bolt. How about that bolt? Hayhanen was asked. In transmitting messages, the former Soviet spy replied, "trick" containers often were employed, such as hollow pencils, pens, screws, batteries and coins. One such object FBI agents found was a hollow 50-markka coin from Finland. Like Jimmy's mysterious nickel, two coins had been used in fashioning the Finnish piece; like Jimmy's nickel, a small hole had been drilled for inserting a needle or some other sharp-pointed instrument in opening it!

Faces brightened around FBI headquarters — patience, that greatest of all virtues in crime detection, was at last reaping rewards. Hayhanen's knowledge of Soviet codes and cryptosystems enabled experts in the FBI Laboratory to break the mystery of the microphotograph Jimmy's nickel had contained. As a sample, one part of this message, which obviously had been intended for Hayhanen, read: "According to your request, we will transmit the formula for the preparation of soft film. . . ."

But the FBI's work in unraveling the dimensions of the Soviet spy ring, of which Hayhanen had been a part, was just beginning. First, who had been "Mikhail," the superior who had "dropped from the scene"? Hayhanen

Left: the "dead drop" in Prospect Park, Brooklyn, N. Y. Right: A close-up of the broken step (now repaired) which was used in 1955 as a depository for messages by espionage agents.

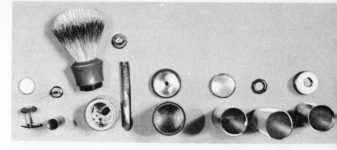

Ordinary-looking utensils (left). The utensils are not quite so "ordinary" when their secret is revealed (right).

could describe him only as a middle-aged man of medium build with dark hair and a long thin nose who gave the impression of service with the Soviet diplomatic corps. The FBI searched through stacks of photographs until they found their man: Mikhail Nikolae-vich Svirin, Soviet representative to the United Nations between 1952 and 1954. Another contact Hayhanen had once used he knew only as "Quebec," an American Army sergeant who at one time had served the United States Embassy in Moscow. The FBI found him also: "Quebec" was Sergeant Roy Rhodes. Svirin was beyond the reach of American justice, but Rhodes was court-martialed and sentenced to five years at hard labor.

Meanwhile "Mark," who undoubtedly still was carrying on espionage within the United States, remained a focus of FBI investigation. Hayhanen provided these clues: he was a colonel in the Soviet State Security Service who had probably been a spy since 1927; he had entered the United States by illegally crossing the Canadian border in 1948 or 1949; he was a man of about fifty, of medium build and perhaps five-feet-ten in height; his hair was thin and gray; he was an accomplished photographer. How did Hayhanen know this last

fact? Once, the former spy replied, Mark had taken him to a storage room where he kept photographic supplies; the building had been near Clark and Fulton Streets in Brooklyn.

FBI agents swung into action; they found a building at 252 Fulton Street and among its tenants was an Emil R. Goldfus, a photographer. Ultimately the FBI by hidden camera obtained a picture of Goldfus, and when Hayhanen saw it, he exclaimed: "You've found him! That's Mark!"

Under FBI surveillance, Mark revealed two identities: Among the tenants at 252 Fulton Street he was known as Goldfus, but when he registered at the Hotel Latham on East 28th Street he used the name of Martin Collins. Arrested for illegally entering the country, Mark became a kind of marvel to the FBI, for the room and shop he occupied "were virtual museums of modern espionage equipment" containing short-wave radios, cipher pads, cameras and film for producing microdots and such "trick" containers as a hollow shaving brush and hollow cuff links. Tried under his real name — Colonel Rudolf Ivanovich Abel — this master Soviet spy was convicted and sentenced on three counts: (1) conspiracy to transmit defense information to the Soviet Union,

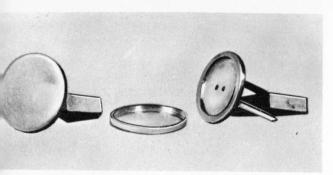

What the well-dressed spy will wear!

Carefully hollowed containers for courier transmittal of microfilm messages to Moscow. All containers were used at one time or another, including the hollow cuff links, and contained vitally classified information.

(2) conspiracy to obtain defense information, and (3) conspiracy to act in the United States as an agent of a foreign government without notification to the Secretary of State.

But the saga of Jimmy's hollow nickel did not really end then, for on February 10, 1962, Colonel Abel was exchanged for Francis Gary Powers, an American U-2 pilot held prisoner by the Soviet Union. Meanwhile, the FBI pressed steadily ahead with its war on other spies.

Another "dead drop" — the bench near Soldiers' and Sailors' Monument, Riverside Park, N. Y. The iron fence was an arm's length away from the bench. A magnetic capsule containing espionage information was attached to the fence and hidden by the grass.

# The Many Faces of Crime

Espionage is only one among approximately 170 different types of investigative matters which the laws place under the jurisdiction of the FBI. Among other major groupings are the following:

*Anti-Racketeering* — all acts of robbery or extortion through the use of force, violence or fear that affect interstate or foreign commerce.

*Atomic Energy Act* — under the criminal section, all attempts or acts to acquire or disclose restricted information "with intent to injure the U. S. or secure an advantage to any foreign nation, or with reason to believe that either might result."

*Bank Robbery and Embezzlement* — the FBI's jurisdiction applies specifically to banks belonging to the Federal Reserve System, banks insured by the Federal Deposit Insurance Corporation, banks organized or operated under Federal laws, Federal Savings and Loan Associations, institutions insured by the

Federal Savings and Loan Insurance Corporation or Federal Credit Unions.

*Bankruptcy* — frauds in bankruptcy proceedings as covered by Federal statutes.

*Bribery* — bribes offered to an employee or agent of the United States "to influence his official action."

*Civil Rights* — discussed separately.

*Crimes on the High Seas* — specifically criminal acts committed on American ships in waters beyond the jurisdiction of an individual state.

*Destruction of Aircraft or Motor Vehicles* — willful acts of destruction (or false threats of destruction) against aircraft or passenger-carrying vehicles engaged in interstate or foreign commerce.

*Extortion* — specifically, where use of the mails is involved to transmit a threat of injury.

IN MEMORY OF
**SPECIAL AGENTS**
OF THE
**FEDERAL BUREAU
OF INVESTIGATION**
WHO HAVE GIVEN THEIR LIVES
IN LINE OF DUTY

| EDWIN C. SHANAHAN | OCT. 11. 1925 |
| PAUL E. REYNOLDS | AUG. 9. 1929 |
| ALBERT L. INGLE | NOV. 24. 1931 |
| RAYMOND J. CAFFREY | JUNE 17. 1933 |
| RUPERT V. SURRATT | OCT. 8. 1933 |
| W. CARTER BAUM | APRIL 22. 1934 |
| HERMAN E. HOLLIS | NOV. 27. 1934 |
| SAMUEL P. COWLEY | NOV. 28. 1934 |
| NELSON B. KLEIN | AUG. 16. 1935 |
| WIMBERLY W. BAKER | APR. 17. 1937 |
| TRUETT E. ROWE | JUNE 1. 1937 |
| WILLIAM R. RAMSEY | MAY 3. 1938 |
| HUBERT J. TREACY, JR. | MARCH 13. 1942 |
| R. E. FOXWORTH | JAN. 15. 1943 |
| HAROLD D. HABERFELD | JAN. 15. 1943 |
| J. CORDES DELWORTH | DEC. 3. 1945 |
| JOSEPH J. BROCK | JULY 26. 1952 |
| J. BRADY MURPHY | SEPT. 26. 1953 |

*Fraud Against the Government* — false claims or the concealment or misrepresentation of facts in cases involving the Federal Government.

*Internal Security* — a correlated part of the FBI's work in combating espionage and subversion.

*Interstate Transportation of Stolen Cattle, Motor Vehicles or Aircraft* — when involved in interstate or foreign commerce, violations include "receiving, concealing, storing, bartering, selling, or disposing of any such [stolen] items, with the knowledge that they have been stolen."

*Interstate Transportation of Stolen Property* — if valued at $5,000 or more and transported with knowledge that the property was stolen; also, transportation of counterfeit or forged securities or state tax stamps or of dies and other tools used in altering or preparing false or counterfeit securities ("receivers" also are liable).

*Interstate Travel or Transportation in Aid of Racketeering Enterprises* — includes both travel and use of the mails to gain a profit from certain unlawful acts or to further these activities.

*Interstate Transportation of Wagering Information* — bet-placing, or information concerning bets, transmitted by wire across state lines.

*Labor-Management* — certain criminal violations committed under the Labor-Management Relations Act of 1947 and the Labor-Management Reporting and Disclosure Act of 1959.

*Piracy of Aircraft and Other Crimes Aboard Aircraft* — to commit aircraft piracy or to assault, intimidate or inter-

Problems of raids, arrests, traffic, etc., are discussed over a scale model of a section of a city at the FBI Academy.

fere with aircraft personnel are Federal offenses; also, to commit aboard an aircraft in flight such crimes as murder, assault, rape and robbery.

*Sabotage*—Generally, the willful destruction or attempted destruction of national defense materials or facilities.

*Theft from Interstate Shipment* — includes theft or embezzlement of goods and the breaking of a seal or lock on an interstate carrier (receivers of stolen goods are also liable).

*Theft of Government Property* — includes theft or embezzlement or receiving such property in the knowledge that it is stolen.

*Unlawful Flight to Avoid Prosecution, Confinement, or Giving Testimony* — specifically, where interstate transportation is involved; the FBI practice is usually to release such fugitives to local authorities for extradition and prosecution or confinement.

Whereas the average American is a thoughtful, decent, hard-working person who leads a well-organized life, without constant vigilance to protect him from criminal activities he would know very little of the "life, liberty and pursuit of happiness" guaranteed under the Constitution.

How commonplace is crime? The FBI has compiled this timetable: 1 murder is committed every 60 minutes, 1 aggravated assault every 4 minutes, 1 burglary every 32 seconds, 1 robbery every 5 minutes, 1 automobile theft every 60 seconds, 1 larceny involving over $50 every 60 seconds, and 1 rape every 32 minutes.

# "The Ten Most Wanted"

To protect his right to a full and decent life, every American must accept the responsibilities that go with freedom. He must recognize the criminal for what he truly is — his personal enemy; and when the opportunity occurs, he must play his reasonable role in the detection and prevention of crime.

Happily, the average American does not shirk this duty. As a case in point, the FBI can cite the record that has been achieved since 1950 when it issued its first list of "Ten Most Wanted Fugitives." By 1965, marking the fifteenth anniversary of this "world's most exclusive male çlub," 194 "top" criminals had been captured — 73 through the assistance of private citizens!

What type of criminal becomes one of the most "ten wanted"? Measured against the average, at the time of his capture he weighs about 164 pounds, stands slightly under five-feet-ten and is thirty-eight years of age. By then he probably has been in and out of jail a number of times, but once placed on the "top ten" list, he has traveled 929 miles in 146½ days before his criminal career ended. He may state, when seized by agents, as did an alleged bank robber and slayer in Philadelphia: "You men are real gentlemen, and if I had to be picked up, I'm glad it was by the FBI." Or, weary and fear-stricken (as has happened in eight cases), he may give up in self-surrender, confessing as one fugitive did in a telephone call in Miami: "Come and get me. I'm tired of running from the FBI." But, far more frequently, cap-

ture requires hard work: there are few short cuts in crime detection.

The ten "most wanted" are not necessarily the ten most successful among criminals; they are simply the ten most vicious, the ten least capable of belonging to human society. Take some recent examples among captives of the FBI:

The Veney brothers, Earl and Samuel, the first brothers ever on the list, were wanted for shooting a Baltimore police lieutenant and killing a police sergeant as part of a bloody Christmas, 1964, spree; Samuel Veney joined the "most wanted" club on February 25, 1965, and his brother Earl on March 5, 1965; both were captured by March 11.

Walter Lee Parman, wanted for a brutal murder in Washington, D.C., entered the club's membership on January

The poster on page 33 is an authentic reproduction of the FBI poster which put George Zavada on the list of "ten most wanted men" on May 6, 1964. Zavada was wanted for bank robbery and as a conditional release violator. It was alleged he had robbed at least six banks in California and was believed responsible for a number of other armed robberies. Zavada was apprehended by FBI agents in San Jose, California, on June 12, 1964. He attempted to avoid arrest by firing at the agents with an automatic pistol, but the agents returned his fire and he was seriously wounded.

On December 29, 1964, in U. S. District Court, Zavada entered a plea of guilty to an indictment charging him with robbery of a bank in Sacramento. On February 3, 1965, he entered a plea of guilty to a charge of assaulting a Federal officer. He was sentenced on that date to ten years on each charge, the sentences to run concurrently with other sentences already imposed. Zavada at that time was already under sentences totaling 46 years for three Los Angeles bank robberies.

# WANTED BY THE FBI

## BANK ROBBERY; CONDITIONAL RELEASE VIOLATOR

# GEORGE ZAVADA

## DESCRIPTION

Born January 16, 1916, Cleveland, Ohio; Height, 5' 5"; Weight, 130 to 140 pounds; Build, medium; Hair, black; Eyes, brown; Complexion, dark; Race, white; Nationality, American; Occupations, automobile salesman, clerk-typist, hospital orderly, laborer, service station attendant, shoe repairman; Scars and marks, scar left eyebrow, scar left cheekbone, scar lower lip, scar under chin, scars on right and left knees. Remarks, may wear glasses.

## CRIMINAL RECORD

Zavada has been convicted of armed robbery, assault and possession of stolen money orders.

## CAUTION

ZAVADA HAS BEEN ARMED IN THE PAST AND REPORTEDLY POSSESSES SEVERAL .32 CALIBER AUTOMATIC PISTOLS. CONSIDER DANGEROUS.

15, 1965, the day the FBI located his automobile in a used-car lot in Youngstown, Ohio; he was arrested sixteen days later in Los Angeles, some 2,900 miles from the scene of his crime.

Gene Thomas Webb, Chicago gangster wanted for crossing state lines in a case of attempted murder and robbery, had the shortest time to enjoy his elevation to the "most wanted" list; he was captured within twenty-four hours.

Thomas Asbury Hadder, wanted for murder in Maryland, was captured while watching a Salvation Army "sing-along" in Oklahoma City; Jesse James Gilbert, California police slayer, despite the disguise of a wig, dark glasses and bandages over a tattoo, could not mislead FBI agents who found him in a street-corner telephone booth in Philadelphia; George Zavada, a notorious bank robber who called himself "The King" and wore a regal monogram on his undershorts, tried shooting his way to freedom against FBI agents and lost; Quay Cleon Kilburn, a prison escapee and one of four individuals twice on the "most wanted" list, learned that an old saying was not quite true — lightning *can* strike twice.

# G-Men in Action

Case studies of G-men in action reveal that in crime detection the patience, courage and persistency of the investigating agent, plus the scientific knowledge and experience of experts in the laboratory, produce the "winning team."

Extortion often tests the full resources of this combination in crime detection, and in terms of public safety extortion can become a game involving extremely high stakes. The FBI grimly faced this fact when they were handed an envelope addressed to Virgil E. Gunlock, Chairman of the Board of the Chicago Transit Authority, and postmarked "Chicago, Ill., Feb. 18, 1959, 6:30 p.m." Within was a typewritten letter, demanding $50,000 "or we will place bombs on some of your busses and trains."

The letter disclosed much about the mind and probable background of the writer. In one passage the extortionist referred to an unsuccessful suit brought against the Transit Authority "to collect damages for injury sustained in an accident with one of your vehicles." It instructed the Authority to "place immediately, an ad*d* in the personal col*um*s of all four Chicago newspapers stating the following:

WE HAVE RECEIVED YOUR INSTRUCTIONS, WE ARE AWAITING *FUTHER* COMMUNICATION. . . ." The letter warned: "It is not our aim to needlessly injure the public, but since your company is public owned, then the public must suffer the consequences if you refuse to pay."

The advertisements were published and brought Mr. Gunlock a second typewritten letter, warning: "If you would rather see an entire city terrorized than pay fifty thousand dollars for your rido*rs* safety, then it shall be done. . . ."

The FBI went into action. Was the extortionist a former employee of the Transit Authority, since his letters revealed a familiarity with company policies and equipment? FBI agents began reviewing personnel files, seeking in particular former employees who had been discharged "under a cloud."

Was the extortionist someone who had sued the Authority and lost a judgment? Attorneys who had handled such cases were asked to search their memories to suggest possible suspects.

In recent months in "Letters to the Editor" in Chicago newspapers, had there been a correspondent expressing grievance toward the Authority? Newspaper files were examined.

Meanwhile, experts in document evidence at the FBI Laboratory had determined from the pica type used that the two letters to Mr. Gunlock had been written on a Remington; the typewriter probably was not in very good mechanical condition.

A number of suspects were interviewed when other communications told Gunlock to await telephone instructions on how and where to deliver the $50,000. The first call on March 5 gave detailed orders of how the driver was to proceed: "If your driver isn't contacted by the time he reaches 63rd Street, he should return." No contact was made; the extortionist was using a "dry run" in order to convince himself that the driver with the money had not been followed by the authorities.

Other telephone orders were received, instructing Gunlock to drive with the money to Chicago Avenue and Hudson Street. "There is a pay telephone on the corner," he was told. "Be there at exactly 9:20 [P.M.]. I will call you at that number." When the call came, within fifteen minutes of the scheduled time, Gunlock was told to listen for a whistle and then to "stop the car and put the money on the sidewalk."

Discreetly, FBI agents followed Gunlock with the money. As Gunlock's car moved toward the prearranged destination, FBI agents noticed a tall, husky man hiding behind a pillar on an overhead highway. The man wore a gray coat, khaki trousers — details relayed to other agents. A shrill whistle pierced the night, but Gunlock, unhearing, drove on.

The man behind the pillar stood motionless and puzzled, until FBI agents poured out of their cars. Pursuit, surrender and a full confession followed for Maurice Laverene Porter. The old Remington typewriter on which all the extortion letters had been written was found at his home in nearby Evanston. He was, as the FBI had suspected, a former employee of the Transit Authority, a bus driver. Tried and convicted, he was sentenced to seven years in prison.

# A Tip Traps a Kidnapper

Kidnapping is a vicious type of crime that has become much less frequent since it has been placed under the jurisdiction of the FBI. The criminal mind of 25-year-old Victor Harry Feguer was simply too immature, however, to grasp this truth: He dared the full manpower and scientific resources of the FBI to find him as a kidnapper and he paid for this folly by hanging by the neck until dead.

It was on a nice day in mid-April of 1960 that young Feguer was released from Michigan State Prison. His wanderings thereafter, as the FBI pieced together the story, carried him to Galion, Ohio, thence to the Chicago suburb of Broadview, and thence to Milwaukee where he purchased a used pistol.

Sometime in July, young Feguer reached Dubuque, Iowa, where, claiming to be a commercial artist on vacation, he rented a room under the assumed name of Sam Newman. He frequented a local bar, was unable to purchase an automobile because the identification he supplied did not satisfy the salesman to whom he presented a personal check, then stole a car that he shortly abandoned after removing identification cards belonging to the owner.

On the evening of July 11 the telephone rang in the Dubuque, Iowa, home of Dr. Edward Roy Bartels. A person who gave his name as Ed Stevens said that his wife needed immediate medical attention; Dr. Bartels agreed to come at once. A subsequent call to the doctor's wife from the same Ed Stevens in-

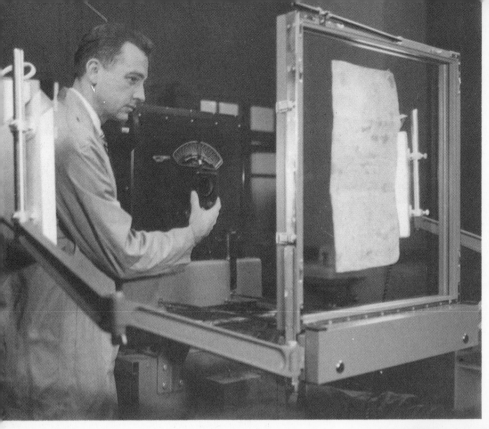

Two burglars gained entry to the second floor of a bank building by jimmying a window. Using sledge hammers, a pickax, and an acetylene torch, they cut through the reinforced concrete over the bank's vault, by-passing the heavy steel door of the vault. As the burglars emerged from the building, laden with loot, they were confronted by a police officer. The officer was shot and killed by the burglars making their getaway.

Special agents found a moneybag in the brush near the point where the getaway car was abandoned. The printing on the bag was obliterated, but through infrared photography the FBI Laboratory determined that the bag did come from the victimized bank. This evidence, together with other evidence uncovered, led to arrest and conviction.

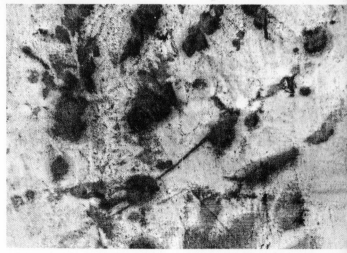

formed her that Mrs. Stevens' condition was so serious a consulting physician had been summoned and her husband expected to remain with Mrs. Stevens all night.

The situation was not unusual for Mrs. Bartels. She spread no alarm until the following day. Weeks later the slain body of Dr. Bartels was found in a small wooded ravine near East Dubuque, Illinois. By then there was a trail of forged checks cashed by a young man who produced a stethoscope to prove he was a medical practitioner.

A name among several on cards left in Dubuque by the fictitious Sam Newman gave the FBI the clue to the kidnapper's identity as Victor Harry Feguer; a photograph of the ex-convict, supplied by Michigan State Prison, was identified as the person who had last been seen with Dr. Bartels. Feguer's

Above: the moneybag, as seen under normal light. Below: the same bag, as seen through infrared photography.

THE FIRST NATIONAL BANK

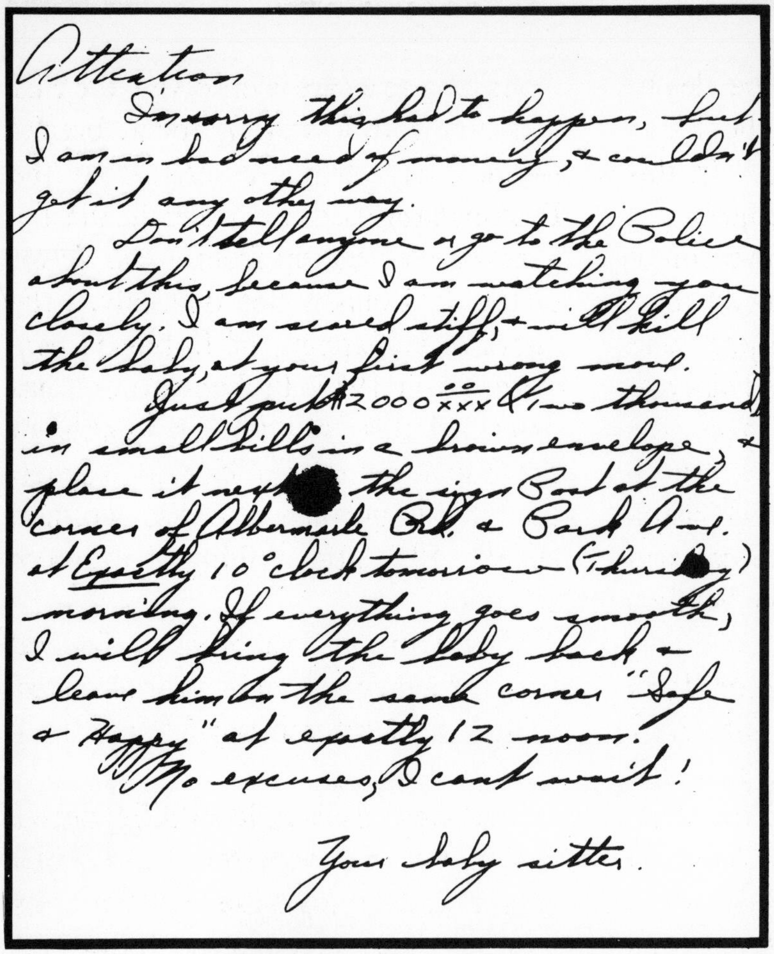

The first ransom note in the Weinberger kidnapping case.

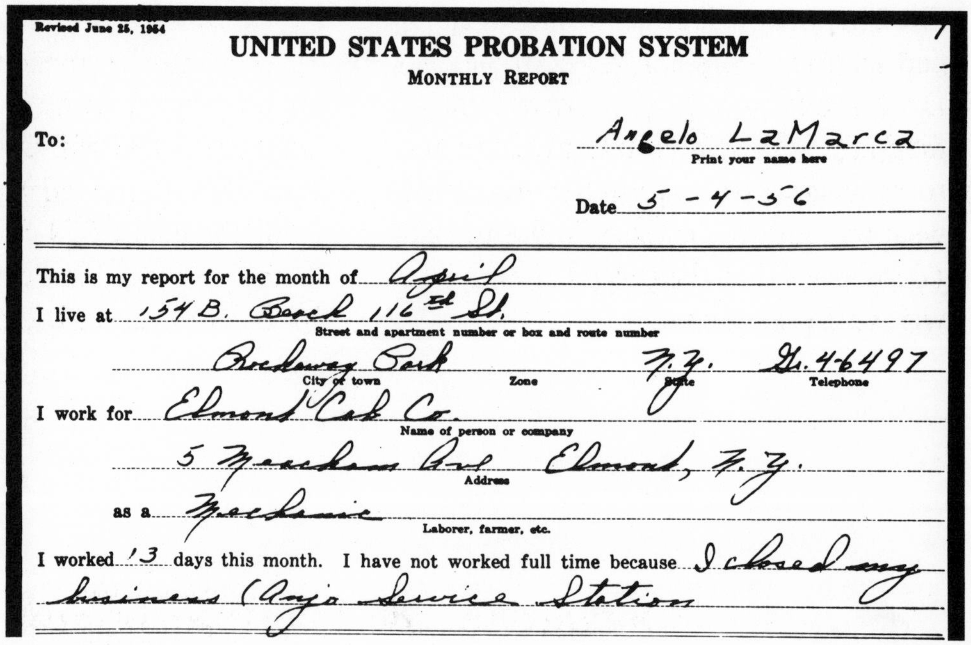

After checking nearly two million records, the FBI found that Angelo John LaMarca's handwriting on a probation report matched the handwriting on the kidnapper's ransom note.

UNITED STATES PROBATION SYSTEM
Monthly Report

Revised June 25, 1954

To: Angelo LaMarca
Print your name here

Date 5-4-56

This is my report for the month of April
I live at 154 B. Beach 116½ St.
Street and apartment number or box and route number
Rockaway Park    N.Y.    GL. 4-6497
City or town    Zone    Route    Telephone
I work for Elmont Cab Co.
Name of person or company
5 Meacham Ave. Elmont, N.Y.
Address
as a Mechanic
Laborer, farmer, etc.
I worked 13 days this month. I have not worked full time because I closed my business (Angi's Service Station

trail from the time he left prison until he bought the weapon in Milwaukee was traced; thereafter the case seemed at a dead end.

But on July 20 the telephone rang in the FBI's office in Birmingham, Alabama. The caller, a dealer on "Used Car Row," was suspicious of a man who wanted to sell him a car at much below market value; the fellow who had offered to sell the car, the dealer thought, resembled one of the FBI's "Ten Most Wanted Fugitives." In this respect the salesman was wrong, but in all other respects the FBI had reason to be grateful for the call from an alert citizen. The car was located and bore Michigan license plates issued only to employees of a municipal or state government, a suspicious circumstance; on a seat was a loaded automatic pistol. The "owner" denied that the car was stolen and gave his name as William Lloyd Howes.

But "the jig was up" for Victor Harry Feguer; he had assumed his last alias. Arrayed against him now were the full resources of the FBI Laboratory that (a) identified spots of human blood on a pair of trousers he had left in a rented room in Gary, Indiana; (b) identified his latent fingerprint in the classified section of a telephone book bearing Dr. Bartels' name; (c) proved that a fired cartridge case, found near the doctor's body, came from the automatic weapon seized in Birmingham; and (d) proved that the forged checks were written by Feguer.

As long as a case is unsolved, the FBI will stick with it, waiting for a "break" — such as the phone call from the Birmingham used-car dealer in the Feguer case, or the tip from a cab driver to the St. Louis police that solved the abortive kidnapping of Bobby Greenlease, Jr. in 1953. Perhaps no one has described this "bulldog"ish quality of the G-man better than Kennie Wagner, the hillbilly gunman who was captured by the FBI after killing five police officers.

"It's a mistake to break a Federal law," Wagner told his prison mates. "They will hunt you down for a thousand years."

The classic example of FBI persistency, of course, occurred in the Weinberger kidnapping case in 1956; the FBI suspected that the kidnapper was a local resident and therefore the handwriting on the ransom notes should match a signature or record somewhere in New York City's vast municipal files; and the FBI proved its theory — after going through 1,974,544 records before it matched the handwriting of Angelo John LaMarca with the ransom letters!

# Outwitting the Bank Robbers

The rapid growth of suburban areas has brought a large increase in the number of branch banks. The dream of quick and easy riches, which constantly haunts the criminal mind, has been vigorously stimulated by this circumstance. A branch bank, staffed by local help new to the business — why, such a place should be a push-over! Or so many criminals have reasoned.

"More and more violations are being perpetrated by individuals with no previous criminal records," Hoover recently told a Congressional committee. "Obviously, these persons, for one reason or another, are obsessed with the desire to obtain large sums of money quickly, but their irrational deeds are virtually doomed to failure. Those who manage to escape from the scene seldom remain at large long enough to enjoy the fruits of their crime."

Years of experience has taught the FBI more about robbing banks than most criminals ever learn. When in November and December of 1962 a total of 152 bank robberies were reported, the FBI found no surprise in the fact that 111 of these cases had been committed by a lone robber. In all, a total of 194 bandits had been involved and within two months 110 were arrested; indeed, in 39 cases the crime had been solved on the day it occurred! The robbery in 1953 of the Franklin National Bank of Franklin Square in Floral Park, New York illustrated how FBI organization has made this type of crime "senseless."

One August morning, as the bank manager was leaving for work, a stranger forced his way into the man's automobile and held a gun against the manager's side.

"Drive to the bank the way you usually do," the stranger said. "There will be a car following us, and there are men already at the bank. I know where your wife and children are, and I have an associate in Boston who, if he doesn't hear from me by 9:00 A.M., will go to them."

How the stranger knew his wife and children were vacationing near Boston was but one of many surprises awaiting the manager on his sixteen-mile drive to the bank that morning. The gunman also knew that the first two tellers nearest the entrance handled the largest sums of money and that the head teller possessed the combination to the vault, which he usually opened at 8:15 A.M.

CHART A

Latent fingerprint left by unknown robber on rear-view mirror of automobile belonging to manager of robbed bank, who was forced to drive robber from the manager's home to the bank prior to robbery.

Right index finger impression of George Patrick McKinney which was subsequently determined to be identical with the latent fingerprint.

CHART B

He knew further that no money had left the bank since the previous afternoon, for he had spent the evening watching the place. His instructions to the manager were explicit: how they were to enter the bank, how the manager was to hold the bag while the tellers dumped in the bundles of cash, how they would depart. No alarm was to be given for five minutes thereafter, he warned, if the tellers wished to see the manager alive again. The robbery worked precisely as planned; it was completed within ten minutes, and the bandit's haul was $190,319.55.

Forced at gunpoint to drive the stranger to an abandoned railroad tunnel, the manager was told to get out and the bandit drove off alone. The car was later found by police a few blocks from the tunnel. A partial latent fingerprint, lifted from the rearview mirror, provided one clue. Another was the chatty bandit's remark that he once had worked in a bank but had quit when "the vice president's daughter got married, and her husband got my job." Thousands of interviews were conducted with banking officials to determine if they could identify an employee who had left his job under such circumstances. Months passed without results.

Meanwhile copies of the partial latent fingerprint were circulated to FBI agents across the country. Almost a year had gone by when one day an FBI agent in New York City routinely memorized information concerning a George Patrick McKinney, aged 27, wanted for fleeing from California in 1952 to avoid prosecution for burglary. Something clicked in the agent's memory. McKin-

ney's physical description, his one-time employment as a bank clerk, his fingerprint all matched those of the lone robber of the Floral Park bank!

At about the same time a woman in Florida, examining the identification of McKinney on a post-office bulletin board, was soon telephoning the FBI's Miami office to report that McKinney resembled a Wade Patrick Johnson, who once had owned an automobile agency in Jacksonville. G-men traced McKinney to a medical center in Jacksonville; he, of course, denied any part in the bank robbery and his wife provided an alibi by declaring they were honeymooning at the time.

But there were contradictions in McKinney's story and the girl's; the FBI kept prodding. A Ronald Everett Martin, who had been a friend of McKinney's in both Florida and New York, led them in turn to Clifford Donald Oberkirch, an acquaintance of Martin's who at one time had been a bookkeeper at the Floral Park bank. Thus the links were forged to trap all three conspirators and send them to jail.

"Tips" to the FBI, vital in the solution of numerous crimes, come from many sources. The woman who noticed the similarity between the posted identification of McKinney and the owner of a Jacksonville automobile agency was surely a heroine in solving a bank robbery that had occurred more than a thousand miles away.

An alert schoolboy in Ohio, sharpening pencils near a classroom window, observed a car careening recklessly into the school parking lot; he pointed out the car and told FBI agents how two

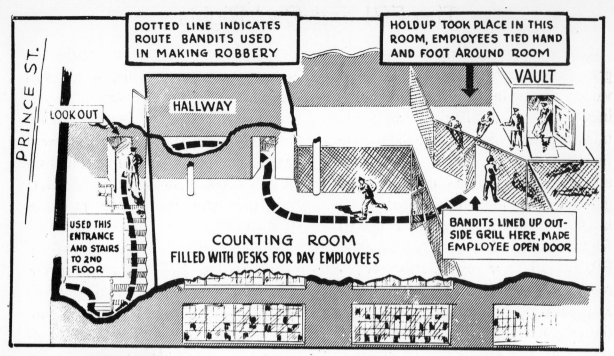

HOLDUP TOOK PLACE IN THIS ROOM, EMPLOYEES TIED HAND AND FOOT AROUND ROOM

VAULT

PRINCE ST.

LOOK OUT

HALLWAY

USED THIS ENTRANCE AND STAIRS TO 2ND FLOOR

COUNTING ROOM FILLED WITH DESKS FOR DAY EMPLOYEES

BANDITS LINED UP OUTSIDE GRILL HERE, MADE EMPLOYEE OPEN DOOR

This diagram shows the second floor of Brink's, Inc., at Boston where a gang of bandits staged the nation's largest cash robbery on January 17, 1950. The eleven men involved netted a total of $1,218,211, but diligent effort by the FBI eventually solved the case.

Joseph J. ("Specs") O'Keefe, member of the gang and chief witness in the state's case against the bandits rounded up by the FBI in the Brink's robbery, returns to jail after testimony.

Wide World Photos.

men had jumped out and ripped off masks. The result of the youngster's tip: the quick apprehension of two gunmen involved in a $31,000 bank robbery.

A different kind of informant eventually solved the so-called "perfect crime" of January 17, 1950, when a group of armed Boston bandits, wearing Halloween-type masks, coolly walked away from Brink's, Inc. with $1,218,211.29

in cash and $1,557,183.83 in checks. The number of "tips" that poured into FBI offices concerning this crime ran into the hundreds; each was checked out carefully, but the field of suspects finally narrowed down to a gang of ten known criminals.

These "birds of a feather" were far from happy once they had flocked together; so bitter had grown their quarrels that three attempts were made upon the life of Joseph James O'Keefe, one of the gang of suspects. Jailed for a probation violation, O'Keefe brooded over his hatred for his former cronies until one day he was ready to strike back by telling all he knew. Of the ten others O'Keefe implicated, two were dead. The remaining eight were apprehended by the FBI, and so, after six years of intensive investigation, the "perfect crime" was foiled.

# The FBI and Civil Rights

Under recent civil rights laws, Congress has charged the FBI with a wide variety of new investigative responsibilities. Complaints alleging police brutality are one type of crime pursued by the Bureau in its efforts to insure for all citizens the rights and privileges guaranteed by the Constitution and the laws of the United States. The Civil Rights Act of 1960 also placed under FBI investigative responsibility crimes resulting from efforts to obstruct Federal court orders by threats or force and the interstate transportation of explosives with the knowledge or intent to employ ·such explosives to damage or destroy any property for "the purpose of interfering with its use for educational, religious, residential, business, charitable, or civic objectives."

"Our investigations," Hoover reported recently to Congress, "have led to the prosecution of many matters in the civil rights field. For example; the investigation growing out of the murder of Medgar Evers, field secretary, National Association for the Advancement of Colored People, who was shot and killed at Jackson, Miss., on June 12, 1963, extended to 48 of our 55 field divisions. As a result of our investigation, a rifle, as well as the telescopic sight on the rifle, which was found in the vicinity of Evers' home was traced to Byron de la Beckwith. Further, the FBI's Identification Division identified a latent fingerprint found on the telescopic sight as being identical with the right index fingerprint of Beckwith."

Not all cases of civil rights investigated by the FBI involve Negroes — in Connecticut, for example, 1963 brought a charge that a Mexican family was being held "in a condition of involuntary servitude" on a farm; the farmer was found guilty and sentenced. In Indiana two local police officers were found guilty of abusing a prisoner.

The fact that civil rights have brought the FBI into bitter conflict with the Ku Klux Klan should surprise no one — G-men long have battled the illegal activities of Klansmen. A classic case occurred in the early 1950's in North Carolina's Columbus County. Here one night hooded Klan terrorists seized a woman and a boarder, and carried the pair across state lines into South Carolina before subjecting their captives to an unmerciful flogging.

During the next three months, fifteen

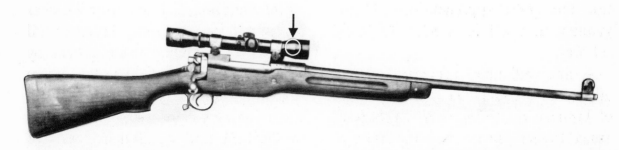

On June 23, 1963, the FBI released this photograph of the rifle which it considered to be the death weapon in the slaying of Medgar Evers. Circle and arrow show spot where fingerprint of Beckwith was found.

floggings by Klansmen were reported and no one who, for any reason, aroused the Klan's ire could feel safe. FBI investigators, of course, were up against an old pattern — Klansmen were protected by their oath of secrecy and by a tendency on the part of their relatives and friends not to talk to "outsiders." The FBI fought back in the only way possible, locating those in the community who were not in sympathy with the Klan's terrorism, offering protection to those willing to supply information. On the morning of February 16, 1952, FBI agents made ten simultaneous arrests of those involved in the first floggings.

Columbus County soon saw an end to Klan harassment because arrest was followed by the conviction of those responsible for the crimes. The FBI was similarly rewarded following its investigation in 1964 of the bombing of the home of Iona Godfrey, a Negro living in Jacksonville, Florida. The culprit in this case was William Sterling Rosecrans, Jr., a 30-year-old Klansman who had participated in the bombing in order "to get out of a white school" Godfrey's six-year-old son. Rosecrans was sentenced to seven years in prison.

Klan activity today operates through four centers. The United Klans of America, headquartered in Birmingham, Alabama, under the leadership of Imperial Wizard Robert Shelton and operating in eight states, may claim as many as 4,600 members; the White Knights of the Ku Klux Klan is exclusively a Mississippi organization with perhaps 2,000 members; the Original Knights of the Ku Klux Klan in Louisiana has about 1,500 adherents; and probably less than 1,000 members belong to the United Florida Ku Klux Klan. It is not numbers but intensity of objective that makes any "hate group" dangerous to civil rights: for example, the American Nazi Party under George Lincoln Rockwell, operating out of Arlington, Virginia, and the National States Rights Party under Edward Fields, operating out of Birmingham, Alabama, probably each have no more than 100 members spreading their doctrines of violent contempt for Jews and Negroes. It is doubtful if any member of this lunatic fringe makes any move, anywhere, at any time without the FBI knowing in advance of his intent.

Still, under law, against these groups the FBI, which is not a national police force, can only function as a fact-finding organization. Recently Director J. Edgar Hoover told Congress: "There are those who would have us ignore legally established jurisdictional lines just to appease pressure groups or others who feel we should be obligated to step in and handle matters which are not in our legal jurisdiction. Ironically, this would strike a blow at the rights, freedom, and liberty of all Americans — the very matter which these detractors claim they wish to protect."

Often wrongdoers in civil rights — even murderers, whose evidence of crime has been well established — are set free by local courts. But at least public opinion is awakened in such cases, and although education may work slowly, it builds solid foundations for a better future society. In an effort to create a healthier climate for this age of America that is emerging, the FBI conducts hundreds of "special civil rights schools" at the request of local police officials where instruction is given in such subjects as the Constitution, the Bill of Rights, rulings pertaining to arrests, searches and seizures, and other legal and investigative aspects of civil rights. Perhaps in time these educational programs will make clear to every citizen why "the FBI handles civil rights cases and all other matters in its jurisdiction without apology to anyone."

# A Career with the FBI

At the close of 1964 the FBI employed 14,565 persons — 6,278 males as special agents and 8,287 men and women as clerks, stenographers and technical assistants. There were 56 field offices located in the major cities of the United States (reaching from Anchorage in Alaska to Miami, Florida, and from Honolulu in Hawaii to Albany, New York); there was a field office in San Juan, serving the Commonwealth of Puerto Rico. In addition, there were approximately 500 resident agencies (or suboffices) scattered throughout the nation; and FBI personnel served in liaison posts in eleven foreign countries.

A boy who wishes a career as an FBI agent must prepare himself to meet certain rigid requirements. He must have reached his twenty-third birthday on the date his application is filed; he must

A special agent takes a photograph of a heel print left at the scene of a crime.

Subsequently, a laboratory expert testifies as to his findings regarding the defendant's heel print and the heel impression.

be a citizen of the United States and willing to serve in any part of the United States or its territorial possessions. He must be a graduate of a state-accredited resident law school or of a four-year resident college with a major in accounting and have at least three years of practical accounting and/or auditing experience. A "resident" school is one requiring personal attendance; and if an applicant is a graduate of a law or accounting school not requiring at least a resident junior college degree as a prerequisite for admission, then he must have received at least such a degree or its equivalent.

There are as well rigid physical requirements. In height an applicant must stand 5 feet, 7 inches without shoes; he must have uncorrected vision of not less than 20/40 in one eye and at least 20/50 in the weaker eye without glasses and at least 20/20 in each eye corrected. He must possess normal color vision and be able to hear ordinary conversation at least 15 feet with each ear. He must be able to perform "strenuous physical exertion" and have no defects which would interfere with his use of firearms or with his "participation in raids, dangerous assignments or defensive tactics."

A boy who plans for a career in law enforcement — especially as an FBI special agent — cannot begin cultivating the right personal habits too early in life. He must have courage, good sense, honest inclinations; he must be a team worker. Sports will help him develop physical fitness and participation in the programs of the Boy Scouts and Boys' Clubs of America will teach him

proper civic and social attitudes. The school safety patrol will give him a good background. And he must be willing to "hit those books" — most of all in such subjects as American history, sociology, psychology, chemistry, physics, criminology, civics and government, English, report writing, business law, economics, public speaking, physical education, typing and shorthand.

Many a special agent has prepared for his career by working for the FBI as a clerk after graduating from high school; in his off hours he has attended professional schools or neighboring universities to meet the full requirements for becoming a G-man. The FBI has openings both for men and women as stenographers or in a number of laboratory positions; and for males only as radio operators and electronic-maintenance technicians. If you can go to Washington, visit FBI headquarters and see for yourself the scope and nature of the Bureau's work. From Monday through Friday, excluding holidays, free guided tours lasting about an hour are offered from 9:15 A.M. to 4:15 P.M. A new tour starts about every ten minutes from the entrance of the Justice

At the Marine Corps Base, Quantico, Va., FBI agents fire at silhouette targets with their pistols.

riodically, veteran agents are given two-week retraining programs. Many subjects are studied: the Constitution, Federal criminal procedures, investigative techniques and the collection, identification and preservation of physical evidence; in addition, thorough training is provided in the use of firearms and defensive tactics. An FBI Academy is maintained in Quantico, Virginia.

Each year the FBI National Academy offers to outstanding law enforcement officers from departments throughout the nation a twelve-week course of intensive instruction and, of course, thousands of other local law enforcement personnel are taught by FBI instructors in their home communities the latest developments in the craft of effective modern crime detection.

Building at 9th Street and Pennsylvania Avenue.

The visitor to FBI Headquarters quickly absorbs the dedication of purpose on the part of employees that has become a Bureau tradition. Training never ceases: New agents receive a fourteen-week course of instruction and, pe-

## Good Business for the Nation

The FBI's unremitting war against crime represents a sound business investment for the nation. In fiscal year 1964, for example, the fines, savings and recoveries resulting from FBI cases amounted to $210,771,402 or a return of $1.43 for each $1.00 of direct funds appropriated to the Bureau. Since 1945 more than 95 per cent of the cases investigated by FBI men and brought before the courts have resulted in convictions. Stolen automobiles recovered by the FBI in fiscal year 1963 numbered 19,192; the following year that figure rose to 19,856.

Under our democratic process, each

year the director of the Bureau must go before a committee of Congress and justify how the Bureau's operations and programs benefit the public. Hard facts must be faced — crime in America is a deeply rooted conspiracy against the public that can only be held in check through constant vigilance. When almost 13,000 convictions result in a single year from cases investigated by the FBI, the staggering dimensions of that conspiracy stand revealed; sentences imposed by the courts in these cases totaled 38,196 years. For the period from 1960 through 1963 a total of 168 law enforcement officers were killed by felons — the courage required to fight crime effectively is no myth.

Nor, for that matter, is the Communist conspiracy against the free world any myth — each year a considerable portion of the director's report to Congress deals with this subject. The FBI reads *Pravda,* and when this official publication of the Soviet Communists devotes a full page to tributes showing "the solidarity of the Soviet Union" with the American Communists, the FBI believes it knows what it is up against. No phase of Communist activity, as it is aimed against the American free system, escapes constant scrutiny: its publications are read, its recruiting activities among young people and Negro groups are followed closely, its "front groups" are pierced, and its espionage efforts are rooted out. Recently the director of the Bureau told his Congressional examiners:

"To counter Communist reasoning we must have a basic understanding of Communist concepts and practices, plus a thorough understanding and appreci-

ation of our own principles, traditions, and objectives. It is vitally important that we know what we stand for and why. This will, of course, give us the dedication and drive we need to counter the Communist challenge in the battle for the minds of men. To counter Communist actions requires rational, calm, constructive, and creative national and international action of our own directed against the root causes of communism, which include ignorance, poverty, disease, economic dislocation, social injustices, racial discrimination, religious anemia, educational deficiencies, and corruption — political, labor, and business."

The primary task of the FBI, as John Edgar Hoover envisions it, is to keep America strong and free, youthful in spirit and alert to the danger of moral decay. He is fond of quoting His Eminence, Francis Cardinal Spellman: "We have no right to expect to keep our freedoms, if we ourselves do not faithfully and thankfully protect the soil and soul of America from those who have abandoned God, and for God's Commandments have substituted their own code of inhumanity, greed, and violence." He is fond also of quoting Astronaut John H. Glenn: "Freedom, devotion to God and country are not things of the past. They will never become old-fashioned."

One good reason why is the fact that the FBI is dedicated to their eternal preservation.

Not all employees of the FBI are special agents or laboratory technicians. A large staff of specialized office workers is part of the complement. Here, one of them operates a machine for reproducing identification records.